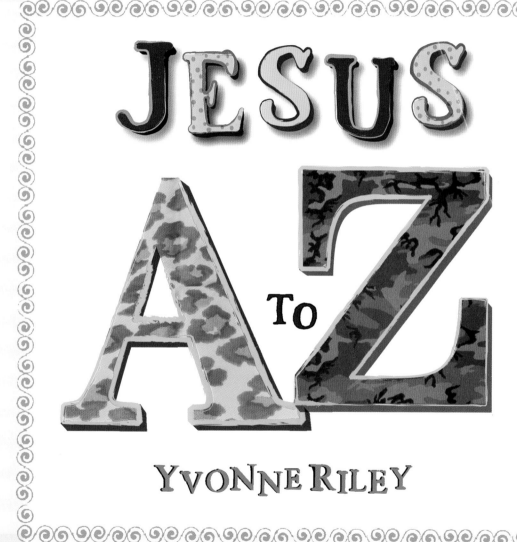

JESUS

A TO Z

YVONNE RILEY

MOODY
PUBLISHERS

Scripture quotations marked NLT are taken from the Holy Bible, New Living Translation, copyright © 1996. Used by permission of Tyndale House Publishers, Inc., Wheaton Illinois 60189, U.S.A. All rights reserved.

Scripture quotations marked NIV are taken from the Holy Bible, New International Version® NIV®. Copyright © 1973, 1978, 1984 by International Bible Society. Used by permission of Zondervan Publishing House. All rights reserved.

Scripture quotations marked NASB are taken from the New American Standard Bible®, © Copyright The Lockman Foundation 1960, 1962, 1963, 1968, 1971, 1972, 1973, 1975, 1977, 1995. Used by permission.

Scripture quotations marked KJV are taken from the King James Version.

Art Direction and Design: David Riley Associates, Newport Beach, CA. rileydra.com
David Riley, Corrie Lauridsen, Jeff Parker
Photography: Steve Anderson

ISBN: 0-8024-2945-9

1 3 5 7 9 10 8 6 4 2

Printed in Italy

THIS BOOK
belongs to:

Alex, Tyler, Justin

Reuter

NOTe to PARenTS

As a mother of two girls, I found there was a need for a book *that could help simplify the truths found in the Bible for children.* A smaller text that would assist me in my pursuit to develop a strong Christian foundation for my girls. And when I could not find one, I wrote *Jesus A to Z* in hopes of filling this gap.

Though there are so many more words and names that can be used to describe Jesus (aside from the ones I have chosen) I believe this is a good starting point for parents, grandparents, Sunday school teachers, or any caregiver to begin developing an understanding in their children of who the Bible says Jesus is.

I have chosen a leopard to take us through the pages of the book because it was my older daughter, Yvette's, favorite animal. She often commented that when she got to heaven she wanted her very own. On April 1, 2000, just two weeks before her eleventh birthday, Yvette died in a car accident and went to live in heaven with Jesus and her leopard. The red tip on the leopard's tail is to remind us of the life

and blood Jesus gave for us and that He took our sins upon Himself. The photos of children in the book are of Yvette, her younger sister, Belle, and their friends.

My prayer is that as you read this book, and hopefully read it over and over, you and your child will continue to grow in the grace and knowledge of who God is— His love for us— His children, and His wonderful plan for our lives.

Yvonne Riley

"Dear Children, keep away from anything that
might take God's place in your hearts."

1 JOHN 5:21 (NLT)

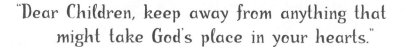

ALMIGHTY

Little children, the first thing I would like to tell you about Jesus is that Jesus is the Almighty God. Jesus is the strongest and mightiest in the world and there is no one greater than He. The Bible says that there are no limits to the Almighty and He is Lord over every ruler and king in the universe.

"But mightier than the violent raging of the seas, mightier than the breakers on the shore — the Lord above is mightier than these."
Psalm 93:4 (NLT)

BeGinninG

Before the beginning of time, God existed in three Persons, God the Father, God the Son, Jesus, and God the Holy Spirit. God has always been here. No one made Him. There was never a moment when God was not God. God never had a beginning, and His life has no ending.

"Before the mountains were created, before you made the earth and the world, you are God, without beginning or end."
Psalm 90:2 (NLT)

CREATOR

Jesus is the one who created the heavens and the earth. He spoke it all into existence by His mighty power. The word *created* means, "made out of nothing." When He created us, God said, "Let us make man in our image, in our likeness." We were created to have a relationship with the Almighty God and to live a life that pleases Him.

"Christ is the one through whom God created everything in heaven and earth."
Colossians 1:16 (NLT)

DiED

Even though Jesus is the Almighty God, who existed from the very beginning and created all things, He chose to become a man and to die on a cross. Because of His great love for us, Jesus died to take our sins away. God put our sins on Jesus so we could be made right with Him. We were guilty but He paid the price by giving up His life. He makes us whole and sets us free from sin. Jesus is the only way back to God.

"For God so loved the world that he gave his only Son, so that everyone who believes in him will not perish but have eternal life."
John 3:16 (NLT)

EVeRLAStiNG

e:

Three days after Jesus died He rose from His grave to live in heaven forever. Jesus offers us this everlasting life that will never end if we put our faith and trust in Him and ask for forgiveness of our sins. God has promised eternal life in heaven to those of us who choose to love and follow Jesus His Son. We are then welcomed as His children into the family of God.

"For My Father's will is that everyone who looks to the Son and believes in him shall have eternal life, and I will raise him up at the last day."
John 6:40 (NIV)

FORGiVEnESS

The reason Jesus had to die for us is that every person, even boys and girls, are born with a sinful nature. Sin is when we do not obey God's rules. It is our own sin that separates us and stops us from being friends with God. Because Jesus was punished for our sins instead of us, we can now become friends with God when we ask Him to forgive our sins.

"We are made right in God's sight when we trust in Jesus to take away our sins. And we all can be saved in this same way, no matter who we are or what we have done."
Romans 3:22 (NLT)

GOOD NEWS

This is the Good News: Jesus loved us so much that He freely gave His own life to make a way back to God. All we have to do is ask Him to forgive us of our sins and to believe and follow Him. Then we will become children of God who will live with Him forever!

"You know the message God sent to the people of Israel, telling the good news of peace through Jesus Christ, who is Lord of all."
Acts 10:36 (NIV)

HOPE

Once we have chosen to believe in Jesus, the next step is to follow Him. We can trust Him with all our needs and desires because He loves us the most. Jesus offers hope, or confidence, that He can take care of us and our future. Why? Because God knows what is best for us and He is good to those who put their hope in Him.

"For I know the plans I have for you," says the Lord. "They are plans for good... to give you a future and a hope."
Jeremiah 29:11 (NLT)

IMAGE OF GOD

Jesus came to this earth so that we could have a better picture of who God is. All that God wants to say about Himself is found in Jesus. When we look at Jesus we see God who cannot be seen. As we look to Him, we see God's plan and purpose in everything He created. We are created in His image for His will and good purpose. Jesus is the reflection of God and the more we keep our eyes on Jesus the more we will become like Him.

"Christ is the visible image of the invisible God. He existed before God made anything at all and is supreme over all creation."
Colossians 1:15 (NLT)

JoY

As we go through life we will experience circumstances that may cause us unhappiness or even sadness. Even when we are sad, we have joy in knowing how much we are loved by God and that we are His children and heirs to His kingdom. Our true joy can only be found in our relationship with Jesus and knowing our future is with Him. No one can take this joy away from us.

"You will show me the way of life, granting me the joy of your presence and the pleasures of living with you forever."
Psalm 16:11 (NLT)

KiNG of KiNGs

Sometime very soon in the future Jesus will come to earth again for a second time. Then, he will be seen for the great King He really is. He is coming to claim final victory over all evil, restore all creation and, judge and reward each person according to how each one has lived for Him. Each one who belongs to Him, He writes that person's name in the Book of Life.

"But when the Son of Man comes in His glory, and all the angels with Him, then He will sit upon His glorious throne."
Matthew 25:31 (NASB)

LAMB of GOD

Jesus showed His great love for us by choosing to die on the cross in our place. Jesus suffered a cruel death because He knew it was the only way for us to get back to God. We were stained by sin, and it is impossible for God to overlook sin. Jesus is the Lamb of God who never sinned, so that He could be a perfect sacrifice. He came to take away the sins of the world. He is as gentle as a lamb but as great and strong as a lion.

"He paid for you with the precious lifeblood of Christ, the sinless, spotless Lamb of God."
1 Peter 1:19 (NLT)

MESSiAH

Messiah is the title for the King that God chose and promised He would send to rescue His people. Messiah means the One "anointed" and empowered by God to deliver His people and establish His kingdom. Jesus is the Messiah, the fulfillment of God's promise – the Chosen One to bring the Good News to us.

"'We have found the Messiah', (that is, the Christ)."
John 1:41 (NIV)

NOBLE LORD

In order for Jesus to become the King of our hearts and rule over us, He must become the Lord of our lives. This means we must surrender ourselves to Him by living to follow Him and always putting Him first, even over our own will and desires. Jesus is noble, loyal, and trustworthy; and because He will never fail us, we can tell Him we trust Him to sit on the throne of our hearts. When He becomes our Lord, we gladly become His servants.

"Then said Jesus unto his disciples, if any man will come after me, let him deny himself, and take up his cross, and follow Me."
Matthew 16:24 (KJV)

ONly OnE

It was God's plan long ago that Jesus would be the Only One who could erase our sins and bring us back into a loving relationship with God. Jesus was born on earth to pay the punishment for our sins and to die in our place. How wonderful it is to know that God Himself died on a cross to save us — His children!

"Jesus told him, 'I am the way, the truth and the life. No one can come to the Father except through me'."
John 14:6 (NLT)

PRiNCE of PeAcE

As God's children we can be certain that the plans that Jesus has for our lives are good. The Bible is full of promises from God that reassure us of His deep love, His desire to keep us safe and close to Him, and His ability to rescue us from any situation that could possibly harm us. When we think about this we realize how blessed we are! He is our Prince who offers us the riches of a perfect peace that cannot be shaken as long as we keep our eyes fixed on Him.

"You will keep in perfect peace all who trust in you, whose thoughts are fixed on you!"
Isaiah 26:3 (NLT)

QuiEt

q:

Jesus had many quiet times alone and away from the crowds when He was on earth. In those quiet moments He prayed to His Father in heaven. He found comfort and strength with God. He also found power–the power to carry out God's will and purpose for His life. God's will for Jesus was to suffer and give up His life for us so that we could be made right with God. Jesus prayed, "Not my will, but yours be done," because He loved us.

"In quietness and confidence will be your strength."
Isaiah 30:15 (NLT)

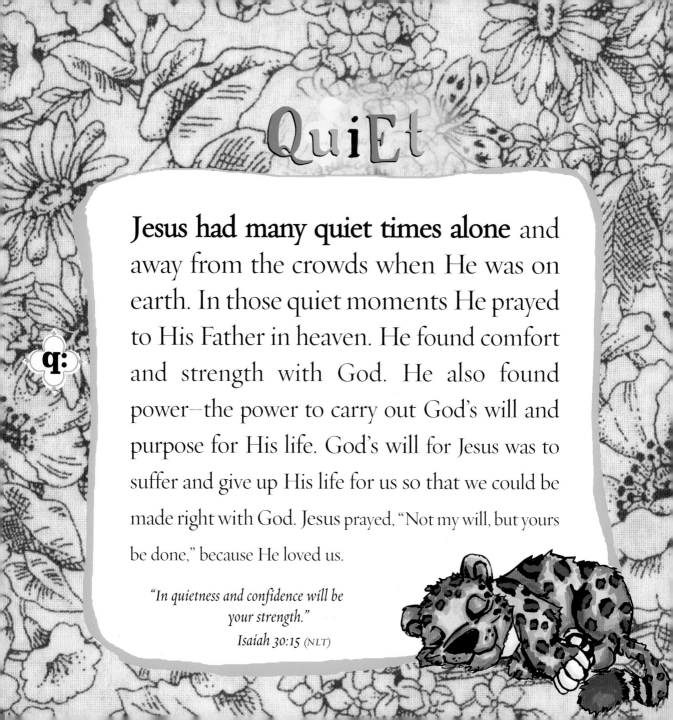

ROCK

The words that Jesus spoke to us are found in the Bible. And if you follow these words, you can build a life on them. You will be like a smart carpenter who builds his house on solid rock protected from the rain and safe from the floods and tornadoes. Hold fast to His words of life that bring wisdom and true happiness. He is our refuge and hiding place.

"He is the Rock, his work is perfect. Everything he does is just and fair.
He is a faithful God who does no wrong."
Deuteronomy 32:4 (NLT)

SoN of GOD

Jesus is the only begotten Son of God. And because of His relationship to God as His Son, He is equal to God and He is God. Jesus has been given the name that is above every other name. Jesus has been honored far beyond anyone or anything else because He is the One True God. After His victory on the cross, He has gone into heaven to be seated at the right hand of His Father and has been crowned with glory.

"The Father and I are one."
John 10:30 (NLT)

TRuTh

God is Light and there is no darkness in Him at all. That means He cannot lie and all of us who love Him realize that what He says in the Bible is true. People who say they love or have fellowship with God should live their lives as Christ did, loving one another with the same love that God loved us with. If we follow after Jesus we also should live as children of light-living in the truth.

"For God is Spirit, so those who worship him must worship in spirit and in truth."
John 4:24 (NLT)

UNdERStAnDinG

u:

When we look to Jesus, we see God's personality: kind, merciful, slow to anger, and so full of unfailing love. Even though we might fail over and over again, He is understanding of our weaknesses. He is quick to forgive us and always ready to welcome us back into His loving arms.

"I am the Lord, the merciful and gracious God. I am slow to anger and rich in unfailing love and faithfulness."
Exodus 34:6 (NLT)

ViCtORioUS

Jesus performed many miracles while He lived on earth. He walked on water, stilled the storm, and healed the sick. But God's greatest work was that Jesus rose from the grave. By doing so He conquered the power of sin and death. He gave us new life and is victoriously seated at the right hand of God in heaven. Now God's children can look forward with great joy to joining Him in His kingdom.

"How we thank God, who gives us victory over sin and death through Jesus Christ our Lord!"
1 Corinthians 15:57 (NLT)

WeEps

Jesus is sad when we push Him away, and His heart is broken over our rejection of Him. There is nothing He desires more than for us to open up our hearts and let Him in. Yes, He is sad and weeps when we choose not to respond to His love for us.

"It is not my heavenly Father's will that even one of these little ones should perish."
Matthew 18:14 (NLT)

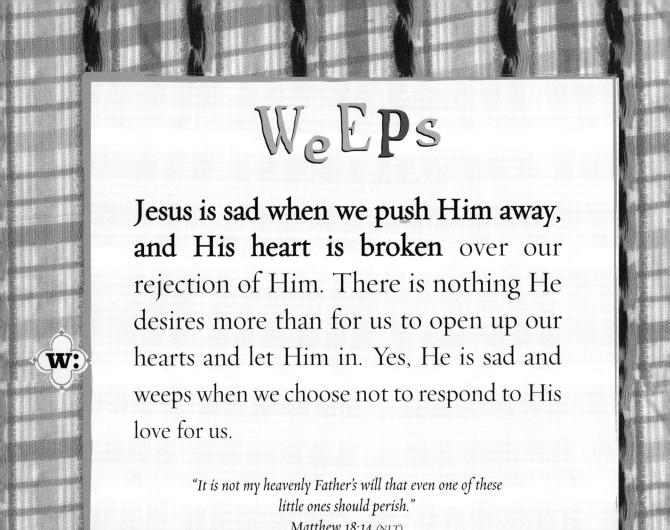

eXAmPLE

As followers of Jesus, we should make it our goal to become more and more like Him. He is our model of love and the eXample of how we should live. When we suffer or are hurt by others, we should still love as He loves. Even though Jesus is equal to God, He demonstrated His love for us when He obediently chose to humble Himself and lay down His life for His friends. He set aside His privileges as God and became man because of His great love for us. This kind of eXample of love is what Jesus wants us to have for others.

"Live a life filled with love for others, following the eXample of Christ, who loved you and gave himself as a sacrifice to take away your sins."
Ephesians 5:2 (NLT)

YAHwEh

The word Yahweh is one of God's names that means "I am" or "the Self-existent One." Jesus is our helper and He is powerful enough to become and provide whatever we need or will ever need. He will always be there for us to help and strengthen us along our way in life. He is our faithful God who guides us. When we are afraid, we can always count on Yahweh in time of need.

"The Lord says, 'I will guide you along the best pathway for your life. I will advise you and watch over you'."
Psalm 32:8 (NLT)

ZEALOUS LOVE

God loves us so much that He gave the greatest and dearest gift, His son. Jesus came to make a way back to God. Jesus paid the debt that we were unable to pay—He gave His sinless life for us. The Holy One was sacrificed in our place. If there had been any other way for us to be forgiven, God would have found it. The cross represents the overwhelming zealous love our God has for us. God will never give up in loving us and desiring our love.

"No greater love has this than a man would lay down His life for His friends."
John 15:13 (NLT)

MORE BiBLE TeRMS

Baptism ~ The outside washing of water that shows other people that God has changed us on the inside and given us a new heart.

Begotten Son ~ The only Son of God; One of a kind in His external union with the Father. When Jesus is called "The only begotten Son of God," it expresses God's love, affection, and intimacy with His Son.

Bible ~ There are 66 different books that make up the Sacred Book. More than 40 authors who were inspired by God to write over a period of 1,500 years.

Book of Life ~ A record found in heaven listing the names of those who have given their lives to Jesus.

Crucifixion ~ The method of torture used by Romans to put Jesus to death. At a crucifixion, the person was nailed or tied to a wooden stake and left to die.

Christ ~ The short form of the name of Jesus Christ, which means the anointed one.

Faith ~ The belief and hope in God and His written Word—the Bible.

The Fall ~ When Adam and Eve, the first man and woman God created, ate the forbidden fruit in the garden that God had warned them not to eat.

Glory ~ Beauty, power or honor; a quality of God's character that emphasizes His greatness and authority.

Grace ~ The undeserved favor, forgiveness and acceptance we receive when we accept Jesus as our Savior.

Heaven ~ The dwelling place and eternal home of God.

Holy ~ Moral and ethical wholeness or perfection; freedom from moral evil. The Hebrew word for "holy" means "sanctified" or "set apart" for divine service.

Holy Spirit ~ The third person of the Trinity.

Humble ~ Free from pride. A humble person focuses more on God and others than on himself.

Miracles ~ Unusual events that reveal the power of God, examples of God's faithfulness and love.

Prayer ~ Conversation with God in which we express our love, praise, needs and concerns with a thankful heart.

Prophet ~ A person who spoke for God and who communicated God's message courageously to God's chosen people.

Redeemer ~ One who frees or delivers another from difficulty, danger, or bondage. Jesus is the ultimate Redeemer; He gave His life to save us.

Resurrection ~ When Jesus rose from the dead on the third day and went to live in heaven.

Sacrifice ~ A substitute payment for our sins.

Satan ~ The personal name of the devil; the great enemy of God and man.

Second Coming ~ Jesus' return to earth to establish His Kingdom.

Trinity ~ The Father, Son, and Holy Spirit are the three persons who makeup the Godhead.

Virgin Birth ~ The way in which Jesus entered human existence.

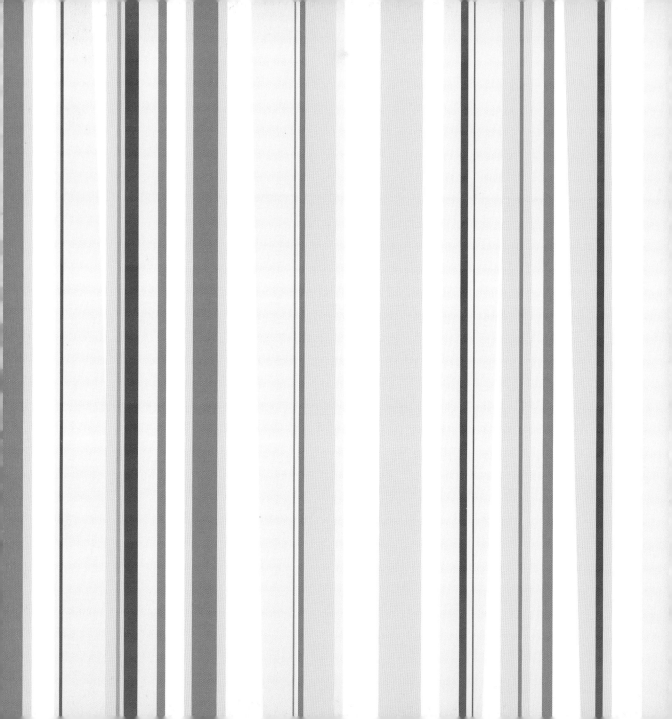

Acknowledgements

I would like to gratefully acknowledge Moody Publishers for partnering with us. It is an honor to be on your team!

Thank You: Pamela for believing in my project, Corrie for the beautiful design, Jeanne, for the first edit, Toni, Nichole, Sherry, Cathe, and Marilyn for all your support. Pastor Chuck Smith for the solid Bible teaching I have received over the past thirty years. Pastor and friend, Greg Laurie, for the inspiration you've been for my life. Sweet Crystal, the songs you've written for this book will bless many. To my loving husband, David, and my precious daughter Belle, thanks so much for your prayers over the years. Finally, my mother, to whom I dedicate this book. You are a living testimony to the power and love of Jesus and the cross.

I LOVE YOU ALL!

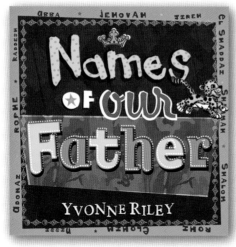
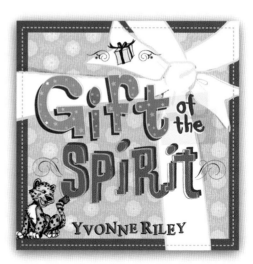

SINCE 1894, Moody Publishers has been dedicated to equip and motivate people to advance the cause of Christ by publishing evangelical Christian literature and other media for all ages, around the world. Because we are a ministry of the Moody Bible Institute of Chicago, a portion of the proceeds from the sale of this book go to train the next generation of Christian leaders.

If we may serve you in any way in your spiritual journey toward understanding Christ and the Christian life, please contact us at www.moodypublishers.com.

"ALL SCRIPTURE IS GOD-BREATHED AND IS USEFUL FOR TEACHING, REBUKING, CORRECTING AND TRAINING IN RIGHTEOUSNESS, SO THAT THE MAN OF GOD MAY BE THOROUGHLY EQUIPPED FOR EVERY GOOD WORK."

—2 TIMOTHY 3:16, 17

MOODY
PUBLISHERS
THE NAME YOU CAN TRUST®

about the
creators...

DAVID and YVONNE RILEY, husband and wife team, collaborated to create this series of children's books focused on the Trinity. Yvonne is a homemaker who writes out of her love for Jesus and children. David is the president and creative director of *David Riley Associates*, an advertising design agency in Newport Beach, CA. They live with their daughter, Belle, and dog, Cosmo in Corona del Mar, CA.